Soul's Reprieve

A Solace for One's Emotions

D

Ukiyoto Publishing

All global publishing rights are held by

Ukiyoto Publishing

Published in 2023

Content Copyright © Dan Pentoja

ISBN 9789360166199

*All rights reserved.
No part of this publication may be reproduced, transmitted, or stored in a retrieval system, in any form by any means, electronic, mechanical, photocopying, recording or otherwise, without the prior permission of the publisher.*

The moral rights of the authors have been asserted.

This is a work of fiction. Names, characters, businesses, places, events, locales, and incidents are either the products of the author's imagination or used in a fictitious manner. Any resemblance to actual persons, living or dead, or actual events is purely coincidental.

This book is sold subject to the condition that it shall not by way of trade or otherwise, be lent, resold, hired out or otherwise circulated, without the publisher's prior consent, in any form of binding or cover other than that in which it is published.

www.ukiyoto.com

To the myriad of emotions one may feel throughout their lifetime

Acknowledgement

I wanted to express my heartfelt thanks to the people who have encouraged me and supported me in all of my endeavors. To those who may come across this collection of poems, I thank you from the bottom of my heart.

Utmost gratitude: To my parents, Lenith and Marcial, who have been with me since day one and have unwaveringly supported me with my decisions. You have nurtured me, guided me, and raised me to be the person that I am now.

To my friends, you have stayed with me and watched me grow. I will always treasure what we have for lifetimes to come.

To everyone else whom I have encountered, I really appreciate the support, the encouragement, and all of the memories we have spent together.

To Ukiyoto Publishing, I am really thankful for the opportunity that you have granted me.

To the Lord God, Our Father, thank you for all of the blessings that you have bestowed upon me. I am forever grateful that I was able to meet such amazing human beings in this universe.

Contents

Turn Back The Time	1
Lonely Steps	2
First Heartbreak	3
Canvas	4
Endless Desert	5
City And Me	6
Awake?	7
My Ilam	8
Goodbye	9
Never Lost	10
Only You	11
The Angel	12
Think	13
Insecurities	14
Smiles And Sleep	15
A.E.J.	17
Beautiful Thorns	20
Free	21
Promise	22
A Mess	23

A Blessing Bestowed	26
Nothing	27
Soul's Reprieve	28
Hurts	29
Arm's Length	30
About the Author	31

Turn Back The Time

If turning back time was possible, then I would've chosen to be selfish and keep you by my side.

If I did, the smiles you're giving out right now wouldn't have been so fake that would put plastics to shame.

Your smiles would've reached your eyes as they twinkle like the stars in the night sky.

Your smiles that I hold so close in this beating heart of mine would've remained so beautiful that would put Aphrodite herself to shame.

Lonely Steps

I'm taking these lonely steps down with the sun as unpleasant thoughts keep running inside of my mind.

I have missed you all day and I know it sounds foolish but I can't stop myself from yearning for your touch.

Why aren't you here with me watching as the sun slowly sets down the horizon and welcoming the calm of the night?

Why am I forced to envision a life without any single trace of you in it?

First Heartbreak

You know I wasn't lying when I said you were my first heartbreak.

I remember that we were quite close when I was young.

Even now, I could still remember your scent.

But then, I guess you really were meant to be the one to break me first before someone else could.

Canvas

Staring blankly at the blank canvas reminds me of my world that has no you in it.

It's devoid of color, it has no purpose, and it has no use.

I tried picking up the paintbrush as I tried to pick up the broken pieces of me that you left behind but I just ended up bleeding more.

Would the color of my blood put some life to the canvas as it drained my own?

I watched in awe as I see you flaunt your masterpiece for the world to see.

It was absolutely beautiful and no words could ever describe the happiness I felt for you.

Then, I watch myself break again for the nth time as I realized the colors will never exist for me anymore.

My love, I'm afraid this canvas will remain blank for the rest of my life.

Endless Desert

I wondered how I managed to live my life before I met such an amazing person like you.

It seems like I've just been wandering through this endless desert hoping that one day I'll be able to find you.

You found me when no one else was looking and you just bulldozed my walls and made me love you more than life itself.

My love, I know I would never feel this intensely with anyone else but you alone.

City And Me

Why did the lights ever go out in the city?

I vividly remember you smiling then suddenly you were gone like a puff of smoke.

I can't exactly pinpoint the exact time when it all changed

One thing for sure is that it was all my fault why I lost you

I spared no effort in living in this dark city all by myself.

But then without you here, it seems like the world has lost the sun.

I tried to find my way back to you and right back to us

But it seems like I'm just running in circles without ever having any opportunity of making it to you

Would the city have the chance of ever having its lights back?

I don't want to hope that I'll be able to find my way back to us then just get it utterly crushed beyond belief.

I can only ask you to forgive me for all of my faults since the day you had the misfortune of meeting me.

If me being me is hurting you then I abhor being human more than anything.

Awake?

Hey, love, are you still awake right now?

Is it alright for me to call you?

I just- I just really want to hear your voice.

I know I'm being selfish but you're the only one who can calm me down.

Hey, love, are you still awake right now?

I just badly want to hear your voice from the other side of the line.

I am absolutely in pieces without you here.

I just- I don't know how to do all of this without you.

My Ilam

I have come to know all those years ago that if it's not with you then I'd rather just keep it all to myself even if it's to the point that it would consume me whole.

It feels like I am carrying the world and all of its sins on my shoulders with no possibility of reprieve.

You have no idea of the anguish my soul is currently feeling knowing that the person I love, the person I want to shower with unconditional affection, does not want it from me.

You have made me into this foolish excuse of a human being just wanting and craving for your attention, for your love, for YOU.

You have cursed me and ruined me for anyone else and I can't for the life of me ever forgive you for making me this way.

I am insanely, irrevocably, and undoubtedly yours, Ilam.

Goodbye

You know that I never ever wanted to say goodbye to you.

Every single time we part ways breaks my heart into millions of unimaginable pieces.

But they say, sometimes, goodbyes are necessary.

Sometimes we have to let go of the very thing that keeps us alive and sane.

Why was heaven so cruel to deny my existence with yours?

Remember that you will always carry with you a part of me as I write this final goodbye to you.

Never Lost

I have been wanting to tell you that you never lost me, my love.

You drowned my soul with such excruciating pain that it was certain I'd die without having any possibility for salvation.

It was difficult for me to fully function after everything has been said and done.

Yet after everything, you have never lost the love and affection that I had for you.

Only You

Every part of me has your name on it

Every question and every confusion that I used to have has been answered by your presence

I always want you in my sight as I can't bear to have you away from me

I can leave everything in my life as long as I get to have you in the end.

The Angel

I promised I'd love you till the end of time

God knows at first sight that you will be my downfall

My beautiful dangerous angel who presides my whole being.

Your existence calling my entire being into yours as the angel finally tempted the devil.

You called out my name as you received your punishment from falling from grace.

You are never afraid of the devil in me, my beautiful dangerous fallen.

Think

I think I'm bound to lose you one way or another.

I told you I was gonna sleep but I was up and I was thinking

About you, about me, and about us

I think it's just gonna hurt so bad.

What am I supposed to do then when everything is just over and done?

I feel like I can't stop anything from ruining what we have right now.

That single thought terrifies me to no end.

You have no idea what it makes me feel and maybe you won't ever have even the slightest bit of clue.

Insecurities

I guess he's not around right now that's why you picked up my call.

Should I drink more?

Should I drink less?

Should I even be in this place knowing you're waiting at home for me?

A lot of people have been handing me drinks after drinks and drowning me from these intrusive thoughts.

I'm starting to hate myself more than I loathe the guy you're with right now.

I'm afraid these insecurities that I have will ruin us in the long run and I won't have the power to stop them from doing so.

Smiles And Sleep

Are you genuinely happy now that we've parted?

You sleep so soundly as I stay awake every night since you left me.

Will you come back even if it's just in my dreams?

I'll try to sleep tonight if you can guarantee that I'll be seeing you in my dream land.

I can't seem to stop the pain from trying to escape my lips that are shut tight.

Alas! It seems that the hold you have on my heart is still as strong as ever.

I was woken up from my deep sleep when I felt the coldness you left on your side of our bed.

It seems I never had even the slightest bit of hope from stopping you.

Who is the reason for that smile you have on your face right now?

Am I already too late?

Or did you even give me a chance to be the reason why you're smiling so happily right now?

I just want to make you smile but why is it so hard to do so?

Is there even hope for me that you'll come back to the safety of my embrace?

Is he still the reason for your smile?

Then, just why are you in that dark corner crying all by yourself?

Tell me, what can I even do to bring that smile back on your face?

He is the reason for your smiles.

He is the reason for your tears.

Maybe, I am the reason why it all fell apart when it all seems to be going all good.

Maybe, I am the reason why you left the bed so cold as I tried to search for your warmth amidst my sleep.

A.E.J.

My world has been falling apart since the day she died and he treated me like I was nothing but a dead man walking.

Music has always been a passion of mine, but lately it felt like music is my escape from reality.

I couldn't see any trace of light in this dark cold world of mine and I am badly in need of it.

All hope seems to be lost not until I saw you reading a book in that quiet little corner of yours looking like a dream.

Don't you know that you're single handedly the most beautiful woman that I have ever known in this cruel world?

Every single thing that you do captivates me and I'm left wondering if I could ever live in a world where there's no you in it.

I am broken beyond repair and I am absolutely terrified that my jagged edges will hurt you if you're ever in a close proximity to me.

But then again, you have this inexplicable pull towards my soul and I can't help but be selfish for once.

I tried to attract your attention by being the best version of myself on that stage but it seems like your attention is somewhere else.

How can I show you the best parts of me when you don't even try to look my way?

How can I show that I like you when you barely even know that I exist?

How can I have you all to myself when it's crystal clear that you want nothing to do with me?

It took time but I had you and it was one of the best moments of my life, but happy moments don't ever last, at least not with me.

Somehow, all the good things that I have and that I treasure had to end and I'm left all alone by myself again wandering in the dark.

I chose to hurt you and them, but one thing you didn't know was that I was hurting myself more because of what I've done.

I lost myself to my demons and I lost you, and somehow that made me lose myself more.

We both tried to fix what was left of us, but we ended up hurting each other to the point that we had no choice but to let go and lose each other.

I want to be deserving of you, of the love that you gave, but how can I be when these broken parts of me keep reminding me that I will never be good enough for you?

I am way too broken for you. I can't keep you close to me and keep on hurting you because I have to protect myself before I get hurt.

One day, maybe we'll find a way back to each other's arms, but I have to fix myself first because I can't keep going like this and I can't keep on losing you.

Beautiful Thorns

It has certainly never been easy for our love to flourish into something beautiful in the world that we currently live in.

The thorns did not just stab me continuously but it also managed to injure you no matter how hard I tried to protect you from it.

Still, you gave me that genuine smile showing no signs of pain and letting the world see how happy and contented you are with me.

I have never been so thankful for the strength you have shown and that encouraged me to endure every single thing if it's to keep that beautiful smile on your face.

Free

Just for a second, can you set this heart of mine who can't seem to stop loving you free?

No matter what I do, no matter what I say, I want to keep holding your hand and beg you not to ever let it go.

But you see, our today already became our yesterday since a very long time ago.

It feels so wrong and so right to just keep on holding to the memory of what was used to be us but there can never be an us anymore.

Promise

If I would've known that the cost of loving you was to bring you pain then I would've stayed away all those lifetimes ago.

I can't bear to be away from you but just the thought of those tears filling your eyes gives me the courage to stay true to the promise I made with you.

This excruciating pain I feel deep within my soul pales in comparison to the pain you'll be going through by loving me again in this lifetime.

My love, it's enough for me to suffer this accursed fate all on my own as long as you are not suffering and that you are genuinely happy.

A Mess

Tonight, I'm all alone in my room looking at the mess I made wondering how I managed to mess it all up between us.

You are that one good thing that has ever happened to me after a series of heartaches and I couldn't for the life of me manage to keep you.

I've said and done a lot of things that I regret, but the top on my list would be how I didn't try hard enough to fight for us.

I should've tried harder, fought harder, just to have you in my life even if I could be nothing more than your acquaintance.

I keep wondering where you are right now and what you're doing and at times I ask for the moon and the stars to whisper to me about your whereabouts.

I long to have you in my arms again just doing nothing but enjoying each other's company and laughing at the silliest things.

I yearn for that gentle touch of your hands and the soft caresses of your fingertips through my hair.

I just need a little more luck, a little more help, and a little more of you to keep me going through this hellish day.

But what am I supposed to do when I miss you so much?

Every single word you have said, every little touch of your fingertips, every single smile, every single frown, every single tear, every single memory of you won't leave my head alone.

What's even worse is that I'm lost on what I could do, what I could say just to have you back here in my embrace.

Our love was never going to be perfect, but it's the kind of love where you have to fight for it and treasure it because it is more than worth it, YOU are more than worth it.

They were right about me not being deserving of such an incredible woman like you.

I mean, look at me, I'm such a mess, losing my head and losing you just because of the issues that I haven't resolved yet.

All this pain I've been carrying has kept me from sleeping well and now that the pain of losing you has weighed on my heart even more, sleep has evaded me until I am left staring at the blank ceiling.

Still, no one is fit to be with you other than me because all of them are lame and you don't need to waste your energy on them.

I am stuck and I can't find any way out of this abyss that I once created to protect myself from getting hurt.

I just want to be with you, stay by your side, love you harder, show you how much you mean the world to me.

But right now, you feel like a million miles away and it's due to what I did and what I said.

I don't care whatever it takes, I'm taking back what is rightfully mine and stop running away from you, from what we once had, and from what we'll have from now on.

A Blessing Bestowed

I have always questioned myself and the universe on what I did to be blessed with an existence such as yours.

It is unnatural for someone like me to receive such a precious gift from the world which is you.

It feels like I somehow managed to trick the whole universe into giving me their most valuable, priceless, and precious pride and joy.

That feeling has not faded even after all these times I have spent with you. Although I might have become jaded, my feelings for you have not and it continues to grow every single second I'm spending with you.

Nothing

Can I wish to go back to those times where everything was all alright and nothing is wrong with my world?

I can slowly feel myself going numb and starting to close itself off.

It seems like there's nothing I can do but move forward on this path that has been laid down for me.

I'm sorry. I miss you. I love you.

Soul's Reprieve

Life is so unbelievably crazy.

One moment, you're just breezing along, and then next, you're slaving out.

It makes me wonder if dandelions ever felt like this when they're blown by the wind to a farther place.

All the scars, the wounds, the bruises that I endured to get to this day was hard fought.

I was always close to losing every single battle but it always seems like I won in the end

Or maybe I lost because I'm still alive and breathing but barely existing.

Either way, my soul needs its reprieve from all the suffering.

Hurts

I am insanely in love with you to the point that my heart feels so full and it hurts.

I find myself constantly gasping for air but at the same time I don't want that sweet relief if it means that I'll love you less.

You see, I am willing to sacrifice my very life for you in its truest form.

If my life is not enough, then I will give you the world, if it's still not enough, then I'll give you the whole universe on the palm of your hand.

It gets harder and harder to breathe and the right words keep on evading me as if mocking me of my inadequacy to tell you just how much you mean to me.

Arm's Length

There are certain things in life where whether you hold too loose or too tight, you're bound to lose the person.

Holding too tight means you're suffocating the person you're holding and it's just going to make them want to break away.

Holding too loose means you're just going to let them slip from your grasp with no way of assuring them that you'll catch them.

I want to break away from that cycle that's why I held you at arm's length, not too loose and not too tight, just enough to keep you with me.

About the Author

D

D appears as an emotionally expressive individual who channels their feelings into writing, providing a much-needed outlet to fully experience their emotions. Currently pursuing a degree in Occupational Therapy, D aspires to aid individuals, whether they have disabilities or not, in regaining their independence in everyday meaningful activities. This commitment showcases a desire to make a positive impact in the lives of others, reinforcing the importance of empathy and support in their journey to improve the well-being and autonomy of those they intend to assist.

www.ingramcontent.com/pod-product-compliance
Lightning Source LLC
LaVergne TN
LVHW041642070526
838199LV00053B/3510